AMAZING ANIMALS
OF THE WORLD ①

Volume 8

Sailfin, Giant — Spider, Black Widow

GROLIER

an imprint of

■SCHOLASTIC

Scholastic Library Publishing

www.scholastic.com/librarypublishing

First published 2008 by Grolier, an imprint of Scholastic Inc.

For information address the publisher: Grolier, Scholastic Library Publishing
90 Old Sherman Turnpike
Danbury, CT 06816

Printed and bound in the U.S.A.

Library of Congress Cataloging-in-Publication Data
Amazing animals of the world 1.
v. cm.
Contents: v. 1. Aardvark-bobcat — v. 2. Bobolink-cottonmouth — v. 3. Coyote-fish, Siamese fighting — v. 4. Fisher-hummingbird, ruby-throated — v. 5. Hyena, brown-mantis, praying — v. 6. Marmoset, common-owl, great horned — v. 7. Owl, pygmy-robin, American — v. 8. Sailfin, giant-spider, black widow — v. 9. Spider, garden-turtle, common musk — v. 10. Turtle, green sea-zebrafish.
Includes bibliographical references and index.
ISBN 0-7172-6225-1; 978-0-7172-6225-0 (set : alk. Paper) - ISBN 0-7172-6226-X; 978-0-7172-6226-7 (v. 1 : alk. paper) - ISBN 0-7172-6227-8; 978-0-7172-6227-4 (v. 2 : alk. paper) - ISBN 0-7172-6228-6; 978-0-7172-6228-1 (v. 3 : alk. paper) - ISBN 0-7172-6229-4; 978-7172-6229-8 (v. 4 : alk. paper) - ISBN 0-7172-6230-8; 978-7172-6230-4 (v. 5 : alk. paper) - ISBN 0-7172-6231-6; 978-7172-6231-1 (v. 6 : alk. paper) - ISBN 0-7172-6232-4; 978-0-7172-6232-8 (v. 7 : alk. paper) - ISBN 0-7172-6233-2; 978-0-7172-6233-5 (v. 8 : alk. paper) - ISBN 0-7172-6234-0; 978-0-7172-6234-2 (v. 9 : alk. paper) - ISBN 0-7172-6235-9; 978-0-7172-6235-9 (v. 10 : alk. paper)
1. Animals—Encyclopedias, Juvenile. I. Grolier Incorporated. II. Title: Amazing animals of the world one.
QL49.A453 2007
590.3—dc22
2007012982

About This Set

Amazing Animals of the World 1 brings you pictures of 400 exciting creatures, and important information about how and where they live.

Each page shows just one species, or individual type, of animal. They all fall into seven main categories, or groups, of animals (classes and phylums scientifically) identified on each page with an icon (picture)—amphibians, arthropods, birds, fish, mammals, other invertebrates, and reptiles. Short explanations of what these group names mean, and other terms used commonly in the set, appear in the Glossary.

Scientists use all kinds of groupings to help them sort out the thousands of types of animals that exist today and once wandered the earth (extinct species). *Kingdoms*, *classes*, *phylums*, *genus*, and *species* are among the key words here that are also explained in the Glossary.

Where animals live is important to know as well. Each of the species in this set lives in a particular place in the world, which you can see outlined on the map on each page. And in those places, the animals tend to favor a particular habitat—an environment the animal finds suitable for life—with food, shelter, and safety from predators that might eat it. There they also find ways to coexist with other animals in the area that might eat somewhat different food, use different homes, and so on.

Each of the main habitats is named on the page and given an icon, or picture, to help you envision it. The habitat names are further defined in the Glossary.

As well as being part of groups like species, animals fall into other categories that help us understand their lives or behavior. You will find these categories in the Glossary, where you will learn about carnivores, herbivores, and other types of animals.

And there is more information you might want about an animal—its size, diet, where it lives, and how it carries on its species—the way it creates its young. All these facts and more appear in the data boxes at the top of each page.

Finally, the set is arranged alphabetically by the most common name of the species. That puts most beetles, for example, together in a group so you can compare them easily.

But some animals' names are not so common, and they don't appear near others like them. For instance, the chamois is a kind of goat or antelope. To find animals that are similar—or to locate any species—look in the Index at the end of each book in the set. It lists all animals by their various names (you will find the Giant South American River Turtle under Turtle, Giant South American River, and also under its other name—Arrau). And you will find all birds, fish, and so on gathered under their broader groupings.

Similarly, smaller like groups appear in the Set Index as well—butterflies include swallowtails and blues, for example.

Table of Contents
Volume 8

Glossary

Amphibians—species usually born from eggs in water or wet places, which change (metamorphose) into land animals. Frogs and salamanders are typical. They breathe through their skin mainly and have no scales.

Arctic and Antarctic—icy, cold, dry areas at the ends of the globe that lack trees but are home to small plants that grow in thawed areas (tundra). Penguins and seals are common inhabitants.

Arthropods—animals with segmented bodies, hard outer skin, and jointed legs, such as spiders and crabs.

Birds—born from eggs, these creatures have wings and often can fly. Eagles, pigeons, and penguins are all birds, though penguins cannot fly through the air.

Carnivores—they are animals that eat other animals. Many species do eat each other sometimes, and a few eat dead animals. Lions kill their prey and eat it, while vultures clean up dead bodies of animals.

Cities, Towns, and Farms—places where people live and have built or used the land and share it with many species. Sometimes these animals live in human homes or just nearby.

Class—part, or division, of a phylum.

Deserts—dry, usually warm areas where animals often are more active on cooler nights or near water sources. Owls, scorpions, and jack rabbits are common in American deserts.

Endangered—some animals in this set are marked as endangered because it is possible they will become extinct soon.

Extinct—these species have died out completely for whatever reason.

Family—part of an order.

Fish—water animals (aquatic) that typically are born from eggs and breathe through gills. Trout and eels are fish, though whales and dolphins are not (they are mammals).

Forests and Mountains—places where evergreen (coniferous) and leaf-shedding (deciduous) trees are common, or that rise in elevation to make cool, separate habitats. Rain forests are different (see below).

Freshwater—lakes, rivers, and the like carry fresh water (unlike Oceans and Shores, where the water is salty). Fish and birds abound, as do insects, frogs, and mammals.

Genus—part of a family.

Grasslands—habitats with few trees and light rainfall. Grasslands often lie between forests and deserts, and they are home to birds, coyotes, antelope, and snakes, as well as many other kinds of animals.

Herbivores—these animals eat mainly plants. Typical are hoofed animals (ungulates) that are common on grasslands, such as antelope or deer. Domestic (nonwild) ones are cows and horses.

Hibernators—species that live in harsh areas with very cold winters slow down their functions then become inactive or dormant.

Invertebrates—animals that lack backbones or internal skeletons. Many, such as insects and shrimp, have hard outer coverings. Clams and worms are also invertebrates.

Kingdom—the largest division of species. All living things are classified in one of the five kingdoms: animals, plants, fungi, protists, and monerans.

Mammals—these creatures usually bear live young and feed them on milk from the mother. A few lay eggs (monotremes like the platypus) or nurse young in a pouch (marsupials like opossums and kangaroos).

Migrators—some species spend different seasons in different places, moving to where more food, warmth, or safety can be found. Birds often do this, sometimes over long distances, but other types of animals also move seasonally, including fish and mammals.

Oceans and Shores—seawater is salty, often deep, and huge. In it live many fish, invertebrates, and some mammals, such as whales and dolphins. On the shore, birds and other creatures often gather.

Order—part of a class.

Phylum—part of a kingdom.

Rain forests—here huge trees grow among many other plants helped by the warm, wet environment. Thousands of species of animals also live in these rich habitats.

Reptiles—these species have scales, have lungs to breathe, and lay eggs or give birth to live young. Dinosaurs are thought to have been reptiles, while today the class includes turtles, snakes, lizards, and crocodiles.

Scientific Name—the genus and species name of a creature in Latin. For instance, *Canis lupus* is the wolf. Scientific names avoid the confusion possible with common names in any one language or across languages.

Species—a group of the same type of living thing. Part of an order.

Subspecies—a variety but quite similar part of a species.

Territorial—many animals mark out and defend a patch of ground as their home area. Birds and mammals may call very small or very large spots their territories.

Vertebrates—animals with backbones and skeletons under their skins.

Giant Sailfin
Poecilia velifera

Length: up to 8 inches (female); up to 6 inches (male)
Diet: mainly algae
Number of Young: up to 100

Home: Yucatán Peninsula, Mexico
Order: killifishes
Family: livebearers and topminnows

 Freshwater

 Fish

© ROBERT MAIER / ANIMALS ANIMALS / EARTH SCENES

Like many fish, the giant sailfin is named for its most distinguishing feature. This is the male's huge dorsal fin (the fin on top of his back). The male is smaller than the female. But with his showy fin and bright colors, he is considerably more noticeable. His chest and belly are a brilliant yellow or orange. The female is a drab grayish white.

Sailfins belong to a family of freshwater fish that give birth to live young. When a male and female mate, the male uses his long tail fin to fertilize his mate's eggs inside her body. The female must remain quite still to allow the male to accomplish this tricky task. She does so by tipping over slightly onto her side. After 28 days the female gives birth. The older and larger the female, the more young she produces.

The giant sailfin is one of the largest in its family. In the wild, it lives in very warm water that is full of green algae. Many sailfins live in lagoons and estuaries that are slightly salty. Others live in freshwater streams and pools near the seashore.

Fish breeders have produced many colorful new varieties of this fish. They are popular aquarium fish. They exist peacefully with their tank mates. However, they must be given proper food and care. A sailfin's tank must be large, warm, and very clean. These fish grow best on a diet of algae and fish flakes. If they are fed too much live food, they won't mature properly.

Atlantic Salmon
Salmo salar

Length: up to 5 feet
Weight: 18 to 55 pounds
Diet: shrimp, herring, and sardines
Number of Eggs: 10,000 to 20,000

Home: North Atlantic Ocean and streams that empty into it
Order: salmons
Family: trouts and salmons

 Oceans and Shores

 Fish

© B. & C. CHERRY / PHOTO RESEARCHERS

The Atlantic salmon is a great traveler whose life begins in fresh water. It stays there for two to three years before reaching the ocean. At four or five years of age, the salmon returns to the water of its youth to reproduce. This return from the sea to the river is called anadromous migration.

The salmon lives most of its life in the cold waters off the North Atlantic Ocean. Food is abundant there. Shrimp, herring, and sardines assure rapid growth. In two years a young salmon reaches a weight of 18 pounds. Oddly enough, the salmon stops feeding as soon as it enters fresh water.

The salmon's return to the rivers of its birth is exhausting. During the trip the salmon loses nearly half its weight. Only a third of the fish reach the upstream spawning places. Spawning time is in November or December. At this time females lay 10,000 to 20,000 eggs. These eggs develop in about three months. They hatch little salmon with white marbled bodies. This stage of a salmon's growth is called a parr. The parr stage lasts a year or two. When a young salmon reaches a length of 6 or 8 inches, it undergoes dramatic changes. Its body becomes spindle shaped. Its bright red spots and dark bars are replaced by a silvery coat. Its coat starts to look like that of an adult salmon. At this stage it is called a smolt. It is now ready to make its journey to the sea.

Chinook Salmon
Oncorhynchus tshawytscha

Length: up to 58 inches
Weight: 10 to 50 pounds
Diet: small fish and crustaceans
Method of Reproduction: egg layer

Home: Pacific Ocean
Order: salmons
Family: trouts and salmons

 Oceans and Shores

 Fish

 ? Endangered Animals

© TOM & PAT LEESON / PHOTO RESEARCHERS

Like other salmon, the chinook variety is famous for its travels. It begins life in a large river, perhaps as much as 600 miles from the sea. The young chinook swims downstream to the salt water, where it remains for four or five years before returning to the place where it was born. Once back home again, the female chinook makes a depression in the gravel on the bottom of the river and lays her eggs. After a male fertilizes them, the female covers the eggs with gravel to protect them. When the eggs are safely hidden, both the male and female chinooks die. Several months later, young chinooks hatch. When the young—called smolts—travel downstream, their bodies undergo changes that prepare them for the move from fresh water to salt water.

Chinooks are the largest salmon—which is why many people call them king salmon. Specimens weighing more than 50 pounds are not unusual. But chinooks typically weigh between 10 and 15 pounds. The number of chinooks has declined greatly, and the species is in danger of becoming extinct.

Fishermen catch adult chinooks as they swim upstream. In some places, chinooks cannot reach their spawning grounds because the path is blocked by dams. Elsewhere, fish ladders help the adults get around dams, but the smolts are killed trying to swim downstream. They are frequently trapped by dams or hacked to death in the turbines of hydroelectric-power plants.

Sockeye Salmon
Oncorhynchus nerka

Length: up to 3 feet
Weight: about 5 pounds
Diet: krill, squid, and small fish
Method of Reproduction: egg layer

Home: Pacific Ocean and lakes and rivers in Oregon, Washington, and British Columbia
Order: salmons
Family: trouts and salmons

  Oceans and Shores

Fish

© NATALIE FOBES / CORBIS

The life history of the sockeye salmon is a tale of heroic effort. Each fall, adult sockeyes swim out of the ocean and fight their way up rivers and streams to reach the same spot where they were born. Biologists don't fully understand how a four-year-old salmon remembers where it was born. The fish seem to be guided by the smell of their home waters. The adults are relentless in their effort to return home to spawn. They will jump over waterfalls and wrestle their way up rapids, never stopping to eat.

When they finally reach their spawning grounds, the male and female sockeyes are battered and weak. They have just enough energy left to mate. The female uses her tail to dig out a nest in the gravel of a small, rapidly flowing stream. The gravel and bubbling water provide an abundance of oxygen, which will be important for the survival of her young. After she deposits her eggs, her mate fertilizes them. A few salmon make it back to the ocean, but most die of exhaustion, their life's work done.

Some populations of sockeye salmon are in danger of disappearing. There are few, if any, left in northern California. The reasons for their decline may include the damming of rivers, which prevents the fish from returning home to spawn. Pollution may also weaken the salmon and interfere with their sense of smell, an important guide to the salmon's spawning ground.

Common Sand Dollar
Echinarachnius parma

Diameter: up to 3 inches
Diet: seaweed and small organic particles
Number of Eggs: thousands

Home: Atlantic and Pacific coasts of North America
Order: sand dollars
Family: typical sand dollars

 Oceans and Shores

 Other Invertebrates

© JEFFREY L. ROTMAN / CORBIS

Common sand dollars are sometimes called sea cakes. They get their shape—which looks like a cookie or a big silver dollar—from their skeleton, which forms a hard, circular shell. The animal has a dense covering of very short, movable spines. It also has many small structures called tube feet. The spines and tube feet give the sand dollar a furry look. Sand dollars live partly buried in sand on the ocean floor. They use their spines and tube feet to pull themselves slowly over or through the sand. Sometimes hundreds or even thousands of sand dollars live packed together in a small area. They may even stand edgewise in the sand.

The sand dollar's mouth is in the center of the body, on the underside of the shell. Five strong teeth surround the mouth. The teeth are used to tear seaweed, which is the sand dollar's main food. Sand dollars also feed on tiny particles of organic matter. In turn the sand dollars are eaten by cod, flounder, and other fish that feed on the ocean floor.

Baby sand dollars do not look like their parents. They do not have skeletons or tube feet. They swim through the water. After a while, they metamorphose and begin to look like their parents, and then settle to the ocean floor.

Common Sandpiper
Tringa hypoleucos

Length: 8 inches
Wingspan: 14 inches
Weight: about 2 ounces
Diet: small aquatic animals
Number of Eggs: usually 4

Home: Europe, Asia, Africa, and Australia
Order: auks, herons, and relatives
Family: sandpipers

Freshwater

Birds

© NIALL BENVIE / CORBIS

The common sandpiper is easy to recognize by its walk. Its tail bobs up and down, up and down. This shorebird lives on the edge of ponds, streams, and other bodies of water. It looks for food at the water's edge. All the while, the back half of its body is moving. Scientists are not sure why the sandpiper does this. It may help to hide the bird against the sound of rippling water. The bird's brown-and-white feathers also help to "hide" it from predators.

Sandpipers depend mainly on their sense of touch to hunt. They use their long, sensitive bill to probe into sand and mud. They look for crabs and other food.

Common sandpipers usually live alone or in small flocks. They join together in larger flocks to migrate. When migrating and when breeding, they can be quite noisy.

Common sandpipers build simple nests in dense clumps of tall grass. The nests are usually close to the water. The parents take turns sitting on the eggs. Sandpiper chicks are born covered with fluffy down feathers. They are active soon after birth. They run around and hunt for food while their parents watch closely. What do they do when they see a hawk or other predator? The youngsters and adults run for cover under rocks or grass. They may even rush into the water and dive out of sight.

Yellow-bellied Sapsucker

Sphyrapicus varius

Length: 8 to 9 inches
Wingspan: 14 to 16 inches
Weight: about 1½ ounces
Diet: tree sap, insects, fruits, and tree buds
Number of Eggs: 4 to 7

Home: North America, West Indies, and Central America
Order: woodpeckers, toucans, and relatives
Family: woodpeckers, wrynecks

 Forests and Mountains

© S. CHARLES BROWN / FRANK LANE PICTURE AGENCY / CORBIS

The yellow-bellied sapsucker spends much of its time on tree trunks and large branches. In this way it is like most members of the woodpecker family. It uses its straight, pointed bill to drill holes through the tree bark. As tree sap fills the holes, the sapsucker laps it up with its long, brush like tongue. The sap attracts insects. And the sapsucker eats these, too. The bark soon heals, so the sapsucker does not permanently damage the tree.

Sapsuckers have another interesting woodpecker habit—they drum. A sapsucker uses its feet and tail to brace itself upright on a tree trunk. Then the bird moves its head rapidly back and forth. It taps the tree trunk with its bill. Sapsuckers also drum on telephone poles, tin roofs, and other objects. Drumming is one way that the birds communicate.

During the winter and while they migrate, yellow-bellied sapsuckers can be seen in many kinds of habitats. But in spring and summer—the breeding season—they prefer forests. The males arrive at the breeding grounds about a week before the females. The nest is usually made in a dead or decaying tree, or in a tree with soft wood. Both parents dig the hole and incubate the eggs. After the young are born, the parents feed them a mixture of sap and insects. They care for them until they are ready to fly on their own.

Bay Scallop
Argopecten irradians

Diameter: up to 4 inches
Diet: suspension feeder (eats microbes and organic waste)
Method of Reproduction: egg layer

Home: Atlantic and Gulf coasts of North America
Order: oysters and relatives
Family: scallops

 Oceans and Shores

 Other Invertebrates

© ANDREW J. MARTINEZ / PHOTO RESEARCHERS

In the Middle Ages, pilgrims to the Holy Land used to drink and eat from seashells. The seashell became their symbol. They called it the Saint-Jacques shell because St. Jacques was the leader of the pilgrims. We know this as the scallop shell. But food lovers everywhere know that "Coquille Saint-Jacques" is a dish made from scallops and usually served in its shell. The shell is made of two grooved parts, called the valves. They are connected by a hinge in the shape of a bow tie.

Scallops live along the Atlantic coast in waters up to 300 feet deep. When the scallop is resting, it lies on the bottom of the ocean. Its two valves open about 1 inch. Through the opening you can see some 60 little round blue eyes. You can also see two rows of tentacles that are constantly moving. It looks as if the scallop is yawning. In fact, it is wide awake and is keeping a good watch over its surroundings. What happens when the scallop locates an enemy? It aims its tentacles toward it. These tentacles can recognize the smell of a starfish. This is the scallop's most dangerous predator. After recognizing a predator, the scallop flees, stirring up a cloud of sand. To move along in the water, it quickly opens and closes it valves several times. This allows them to clack together. When the valves separate, water enters the shell. When they close, the water is thrust out with force. This propels the animal in the opposite direction.

12

Sea Fan
Gorgonia ventalina

Height: 1 foot
Width: 1¼ feet
Diet: fish and crustaceans
Number of Young: 1 larva
Home: western Mediterranean
Sea and eastern Atlantic
Ocean

Order: sea fans, sea feathers,
and relatives
Family: sea fans

Oceans and
Shores

Other
Invertebrates

© CHRISTIAN QUILLIVIC / BIOS / PETER ARNOLD, INC.

With their branches swaying in the ocean water, a group of sea fans looks much like a windswept grove of miniature trees. But like other coral, sea fans aren't plants at all. Plants can make their food from sunlight. The sea fan must capture its food as other animals do.

Since a sea fan is rooted permanently in one place, it must wait for prey to come near. Then, when a fish swims by, the sea fan shoots out a tiny stinging harpoon. This stabs and paralyzes the fish. The sea fan draws the stunned prey in and slowly absorbs the fish directly into its body.

The sea fan grows very slowly. Its branches gradually lengthen and sprout smaller "twigs." These branches always stay in the same place. That is, this animal remains perfectly flat—like a paper fan. When it's time to reproduce, a sea fan fertilizes its own egg and releases it into the water. Almost instantly, the egg grows into a long larva, which floats for a few hours before settling onto the ocean floor. The larva then slowly grows into an adult sea fan. Divers often snap off sea fans and sell them as souvenirs in tourist shops. This is an unfortunate trend, however. Sea fans grow slowly—less than ½ inch a year. Collecting them can seriously reduce their numbers. The message for divers should be: "Look, but don't touch!"

Common Sea Horse
Hippocampus guttulatus

Length: about 4 inches
Diet: zooplankton and shrimp
Method of Reproduction:
  live-bearer

Home: Mediterranean coasts
  of Europe
Order: pipefishes, sticklebacks
Family: pipefishes, seahorses

 Oceans and Shores

Fish

© REINHARD DIRSCHERL / BIOS / PETER ARNOLD, INC.

The sea horse hardly looks like a fish. Its genus name describes it best. *Hippocampus* means "horse-caterpillar." The sea horse has a horsey-looking snout. The snout is actually a long feeding tube. The creature uses this tube like a vacuum cleaner. It sucks plankton and small shrimp off sea grass.

The sea horse's strange shape has inspired many legends. Ancient Romans and Greeks made potions out of sea horses. They believed the potions could do anything. They were used to help people fall in love. They were even used to cure baldness! The truth about sea horses is even more fantastic. It is the male sea horse who gets "pregnant."

During courtship, common sea horses hold tails. They look like teenagers in love.

They are the only sea horses with this romantic habit. Why do they hold tails? Because it keeps common sea horses from mating with the wrong species. Common sea horses share their home with short-nosed sea horses. The two species look very much alike. But short-nosed sea horses do not hold tails.

The male sea horse has a special brood pouch. He bows and bends to persuade a female to deposit her eggs in it. There the eggs are fertilized and develop. When the eggs hatch, the father sea horse pumps his C-shaped body like an accordion. This pushes the baby sea horses out of the pouch and into the sea.

California Sea Lion
Zalophus californianus

Length: 6 to 8 feet (male); 5 to 6½ feet (female)
Weight: 440 to 660 pounds (male); 100 to 220 pounds (female)
Number of Young: 1

Diet: squid, octopus, and fish
Home: Pacific coast of North America
Order: carnivores
Family: eared seals, sea lions

 Oceans and Shores

 Mammals

© TIM DAVIS / CORBIS

The California sea lion is the smallest of the sea lion family. It is perhaps most familiar as the "performing seal" at circuses. It is by nature playful and curious. In the wild it throws fish and other objects and catches them with its nose.

California sea lions are both the smallest and fastest sea lions in the world. They are excellent swimmers and divers. They can descend to depths of 450 feet. And they can swim as fast as 25 miles per hour. They are excellent fishermen. In murky water, they use their long whiskers and a type of sonar to detect prey. Outside of the breeding season, they live on rocky shores. They live in large mixed herds called rookeries. They migrate north in winter but return south when the sea freezes.

The breeding season is May and June. At this time the males, called bulls, establish their territories. They also gather a harem of 10 to 20 females, called cows. Each cow gives birth to one blue-eyed pup. She nurses it for up to a year.

California sea lions were once killed for their blubber. The blubber contained valuable oil. They were also hunted for their meat. This was used to make dog food. California sea lions are not officially endangered. But they are protected by law. And their once-reduced populations are recovering.

Common Sea Star
Asterias rubens

Width: generally 4 to 6 inches—often as much as 20 inches
Diet: mollusks, such as clams and oysters
Method of Reproduction: egg layer

Home: north Atlantic coasts and Mediterranean Sea
Order: sea stars
Family: sea stars

 Oceans and Shores

 Other Invertebrates

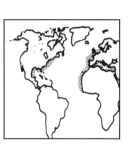

© ROBERT YIN / CORBIS

Sea stars are commonly called starfish. But biologists call them sea stars because these strange animals are not at all like fish. Their relatives are sea lilies, sand dollars, sea urchins, and sea cucumbers.

The common sea star is most often found in Europe. A very similar one, *Asterias forbesi*, is found along the Atlantic coast of the United States. Like most sea stars, *Asterias* lives in tidal zones. It stays on rocks, in the sand, or in tidal pools at low tide. It can even stay out of water for a rather long period of time. The sea star's body has a rugged look, and its back is dotted with short spines. In a groove on the bottom of each of its five arms are dozens of "tube feet," which have suckers on the ends. These suckers help it move and cling to its surroundings. *Asterias* have five thick arms. The arms often break off at the base if a predator grabs one. The lost arm grows again little by little, so sea stars are often found with one arm shorter than the others.

Sea stars digest mussels and oysters in a strange way. They wrap mussel or oysters shells in their arms and then pull open the two parts of the shell using their tube feet. They squeeze very tightly until the muscle of the shellfish tires out. The sea star then turns its stomach inside out and puts it into the open shell. The sea star eats its prey while the shellfish is still in the shell.

Edible Sea Urchin
Echinus esculentus

Length: up to 7 inches
Diet: algae and decaying animal matter
Method of Reproduction: egg layer

Home: northeastern Atlantic Ocean
Order: sea urchins
Family: edible sea urchins

 Oceans and Shores

 Other Invertebrates

© JEFFREY L. ROTMAN / CORBIS

The edible sea urchin is harvested for its eggs, or "caviar." Many Europeans consider the caviar from this species to be a gourmet delicacy. The edible sea urchin can be broken open and its contents cooked, or its eggs can be eaten raw.

The edible sea urchin protects itself from its nonhuman enemies—sea stars and fish—with a large number of sharp and slender spines. The spines can move in all directions because they are attached to the urchin's skeleton by flexible joints. In between the spines are tall, movable stalks that end in tiny pinchers. The urchin uses them to nip at its enemies and to catch bits of floating food.

Edible sea urchins prefer relatively shallow waters near the European coast. Like other sea urchins, this species lives on rocks, where it feeds on algae and decaying animals. It scrapes its food from the rocks using its small mouth and five sharp teeth. The urchin's mouth is located, like a belly button, at the center of its underside.

When edible sea urchins die, their spines and stalks fall off, and their round skeletons may wash ashore. A sea-urchin skeleton, or "test," looks like a decorated doorknob with patterns of lines and bumps. These delicate shells are often sold in curio shops.

Bearded Seal
Erignathus barbatus

Length: 7 to 9 feet
Weight: 450 to 800 pounds
Diet: crabs, shrimps, clams, cod, and flounder
Number of Young: 1

Home: Arctic Ocean and adjoining seas
Order: carnivores
Family: earless seals, true seals

  Arctic and Antarctic

Mammals

© DOUG ALLAN / PHOTO RESEARCHERS

The bearded seal slowly glides its sleek body through the deep, cold Arctic waters. Its glistening, long white whiskers brush against the ocean floor. It is feeling for tiny morsels of food.

The bearded seal is named for its decorative mustache. But it could also have been named the "singing seal." It's one of the few species that can carry a fine tune. Many species of seal whistle, chirp, and trill from time to time. They often do this to call a lost pup. But the bearded seal's special song is long and melodic. Its melodies always end with a moaning sound.

The male bearded seal dives hundreds of feet to the ocean depths. It sings a crazy tune as it dives. At the same time, it releases a long burst of air bubbles. These slowly spiral up to the surface. This is the male's love song. He uses it to persuade a female to become his mate. His loud singing also warns other males to keep away from his territory. Each seal has its own individual song. These songs help seals recognize who and where their neighbors are.

Eskimo who hunt the seals listen for their songs. How do they do this? They place a kayak paddle into the water. Then they press an ear against the end of the paddle. They use the bearded seal's skin to make harpoon lines for walrus hunting.

Gray Seal
Halichoerus grypus

Length: up to 9 feet
Weight: up to 660 pounds
Diet: mainly fish
Number of Young: 1
Home: North Atlantic Ocean and Baltic Sea

Order: carnivores
Family: earless seals, true seals

  Oceans and Shores

Mammals

© TONY HAMBLIN / CORBIS

The gray seal is a large mammal. It has a streamlined body that glides easily through the sea. This friendly animal has keen eyesight and excellent hearing. A strong swimmer, it uses its back flippers to propel itself. The gray seal can also dive to great depths. It hunts near coasts and the mouths of rivers. Its favorite foods are cod, salmon, herring, and other fish. Sometimes it also eats squid and crabs. Its main enemy is the killer whale.

The gray seal is an odd-looking creature. Its neck is bulky and fat, with three folds of skin. The front flippers are short, with long, curved claws. The rear flippers are always turned backward. This makes traveling on land difficult, but not impossible. Male gray seals are larger and heavier than females. Males and females also have different coats. The male's coat is dark with bright spots. The female's is bright with dark spots. Gray seals usually gather in large groups during the breeding season. Each male claims a territory. The male shares his territory with about six females. Offspring are born about 11 months after mating. Young gray seals are covered with coats of long white fur. They nurse for about three weeks. During this time the young usually remain on land, even though they are able to swim. They grow rapidly. At birth a gray seal weighs about 33 pounds. By the time it is weaned, it weighs about 110 pounds. Gray seals can live for more than 40 years.

Harbor Seal
Phoca vitulina

Length: up to 6 feet
Weight: 100 to 400 pounds or more
Diet: fish and squid
Number of Young: 1 or 2
Home: coastal waters off North America, Europe, and Asia

Order: carnivores
Family: earless seals, true seals

 Oceans and Shores

 Mammals

© JOE MCDONALD / CORBIS

Harbor seals are built for life in the water. They are graceful and powerful swimmers. They use their large hind limbs to push themselves through the water. They use their small front limbs to steer. Harbor seals cannot turn their hind limbs forward. So "normal" land travel is impossible for them. On land, they travel by wiggling and hunching their bodies. Imagine yourself sitting on the floor of a room. Now try to get across the room without using your arms or legs. That's how this seal gets around on land!

The harbor seal's body is covered with a coat of short, coarse hair. Under the skin is a thick layer of fat. The fat is called blubber. Blubber insulates the seal from the cold. It also is a reserve food source. When food is scarce, the seal's body burns blubber for energy.

Harbor seals spend most of their time in shallow water and on land. They are often found near the mouths of large rivers. Sometimes they wander many miles upstream. Their main enemies are sharks, killer whales, and people.

Harbor seals mate in the sea. But the female gives birth on land. She usually has one offspring, or pup, at a time. The newborn pup weighs about 22 pounds. It is about 30 inches long. Like all mammals, harbor seals nurse their young. A pup nurses for four to six weeks. Then the mother sends the pup away. The young seal must survive on its own.

Harp Seal
Pagophilus groenlandicus

Length: up to 6½ feet
Weight: up to 330 pounds
Diet: mainly fish and crabs
Number of Young: 1
Home: northern Atlantic and Arctic oceans

Order: carnivores
Family: earless seals, true seals

 Oceans and Shores

 Mammals

© KEVIN SCHAFER / CORBIS

The sweet baby face of the newborn harp seal has captured the hearts of millions and helped inspire the environmental movement. Although harp seals are not in danger of extinction, people have strongly protested the brutal slaughter of harp seal pups.

Harp seals give birth on ice floes near Newfoundland, Canada, and in the White Sea, north of Russia. The mothers nurse their pups for about 12 days and then leave to go fishing. The babies remain behind, camouflaged against the snow and ice by their downy white coats. They can't join their parents in the water for about a month, when their baby fur is replaced by a dark, waterproof coat.

During this first month of life, baby harp seals are hunted by club-wielding fur trappers. The hunters have clubbed many thousands of the helpless newborn seals each year. To stop the slaughter, animal defenders began spraying dye on the pups' fur. This spoils the white coats for fur making but saves the lives of many baby harp seals each year.

Harp seals that survive to adulthood are ready to mate when they are 5 or 6 years old. As far as scientists can tell, mated couples stay together for life. Harp seals that avoid being eaten by killer whales and sharks can live for 30 years or more.

Northern Elephant Seal
Mirounga angustirostris

Length: 14 to 21 feet (male);
10 to 11½ feet (female)
Weight: up to 7,700 pounds
(male); up to 2,000 pounds
(female)
Diet: fish and squid

Number of Young: 1
Home: North America
Order: carnivores
Family: earless seals, true
seals

 Oceans and Shores

 Mammals

© HAL BERAL / CORBIS

Elephant seals get their name from the male's huge nose. This "trunk" may be up to 1½ feet long! Most of the time, the nose hangs limply over the mouth. But when the seal wants to look fierce, it inflates the nose and roars loudly. The noise can be heard up to a mile away.

Male elephant seals often inflate their nose and roar to threaten other male elephant seals. The males threaten one another over territory and over females. If threats do not work, the males fight. They charge into one another and use their canine teeth as weapons. Many of the males are covered with scars as a result of their fights.

Elephant seals are excellent swimmers and divers. They may dive to depths of 200 feet or more in search of prey. These mammals are clumsy on land, but they spend quite a lot of time ashore. Once a year the elephant seals molt, shedding their coat of short, coarse fur. The fur and the outer layer of skin fall off in big patches, revealing bright, pink skin. The elephant seals do not eat while they molt.

Female elephant seals give birth in December or January. A baby, or pup, weighs about 65 pounds at birth. It feeds on its mother's milk, which contains more fat—54 percent, to be exact—than the milk of any other mammal. By the time the pup is a month old, it weighs about 400 pounds!

Northern Fur Seal
Callorhinus ursinus

Length: about 7 feet (male);
about 4½ feet (female)
Weight: up to 595 pounds
(male); up to 110 pounds
(female)
Number of Young: 1

Diet: squid and fish
Home: coastal waters of the
northern Pacific Ocean
Order: carnivores
Family: eared seals, sea lions

Oceans and
Shores

Mammals

© ROY CORRAL / CORBIS

The northern fur seal, or Alaskan fur seal, is a conservation success story. By the turn of the century, it had been nearly wiped out by hunters who shot the seals as they swam in the ocean. Several million were killed for their thickly furred pelts. By 1911 very few northern fur seals were left for hunting. With the creature critically endangered, the countries of the world agreed to stop the slaughter. Today the northern fur seal has recovered and may number nearly 2 million.

The northern fur seal is unique among seals in that it spends almost all its time at sea. It can survive in frigid waters because of its heavy fur and a thick layer of fat. In winter, northern fur seals migrate hundreds or even thousands of miles. In May, males

old enough to mate return to the islands where they were born. Once they have landed, the males will neither eat nor drink for months. They fight, bellow, and call to stake their territories and wait for their "wives." The female fur seals arrive in June. They each give birth to one pup, which was conceived the year before. A female northern fur seal stays with her pup for just one week after it's born. She then dives into the sea to hunt, leaving her baby to play and sleep with the other pups. She returns to feed it just once a week. Amazingly, though the rock beach may be crowded with thousands of seals, each mother will be able to find her pup by its unique call, appearance, and smell.

Blue Shark
Prionace glauca

Length: usually 11 feet or less
Weight: up to 440 pounds
Diet: mainly fish and squid
Number of Young: up to 80

Home: tropical and temperate oceans around the world
Order: ground sharks
Family: requiem sharks

 Oceans and Shores

 Fish

© AMOS NACHOUM / CORBIS

The blue shark has a deadly set of large, razor-sharp teeth. The creature usually preys on small schooling fish such as herring, mackerel, and sardines. But it attacks any animal it sees, including other sharks. It even follows ships to feed on garbage thrown overboard.

Blue sharks usually live in the open ocean far from shore. Therefore, swimmers seldom encounter these terrifying fish. But blue sharks can be dangerous, particularly when people fall or jump overboard following ship accidents. The fish also have been known to bother skin divers. Fishermen dislike blue sharks because the animals attack filled nets, tearing apart the nets to get at the freshly caught fish.

These sharks have a slim, streamlined body with a long, pointed snout. They are blue on the upper surface and have a white belly. Like all sharks, blues cannot float because they do not have an organ called the swim bladder. Therefore, they must constantly swim—even when they sleep. They often swim slowly at the water's surface. But when they sense food, they move quickly. Blues have been clocked at speeds of more than 20 miles per hour.

Blue sharks migrate, swimming toward the poles in summer, and returning to warmer waters for the winter. During these migrations, they follow schools of fish that serve as a constant source of food.

Great White Shark
Carcharodon carcharias

Length: up to 23 feet (record: 39 feet)
Weight: up to 3 tons
Diet: carnivorous
Number of Young: 1

Home: tropical and temperate oceans
Order: mackerel sharks
Family: mackerel sharks, porbeagles

 Oceans and Shores

 Fish

© STEPHEN FRINK / GETTY IMAGES

The great white shark is a predatory fish. It has a scary reputation. Many people fear it because of attacks on human swimmers. The great white is recognized by the large fin on its back. The fin has a triangular shape. The shark has a pointed snout with frightening jaws. It has a large black spot behind the fins on its chest. The shark's large teeth give it a menacing appearance. They are as sharp as razor blades. The teeth are arranged in several rows. They can reach 3 inches in length. Sometimes a shark loses a tooth. When this happens, another one is ready to replace it.

The great white shark is actually gray blue in color. It can be found in all the warm seas. It is especially common in the waters off Australia. It generally lives in the high seas. It rarely goes near the coast. The great white shark usually feeds on the remains of dead animals. But it is considered to be very dangerous. The great white has often been called a "man-eater." A shark's bite can be fatal. However, it rarely attacks people. Human bodies have been discovered in the stomachs of some sharks. So have seals, other sharks, tin cans, and jars. Yet the great white shark really prefers to eat crustaceans, mollusks, and fish.

The great white spends much of its time drifting through the water. But when it wants to, it can reach a speed of 25 miles per hour.

Nurse Shark
Ginglymostoma cirratum

Length: 10 to 14 feet
Weight: 600 to 1,000 pounds
Diet: prawns, lobsters, cuttlefish, and sea urchins
Number of Young: 4 to 8

Home: warm waters throughout the world
Order: carpet sharks
Family: nurse sharks

Oceans and Shores

Fish

No one is really sure how the nurse shark got its name. Some marine biologists (scientists who study sea life) say that the creature looks like it is "nursing" a bottle when it sucks a fish into its mouth, headfirst. Some fishermen tell stories about nurse sharks helping, or "nursing," other injured sharks. But scientists say this fish tale is pure fantasy.

The nurse shark is a drab, slow-moving creature. It is often spotted lying very still under the outcroppings of a coral reef. It has a reputation for being gentle—compared with other sharks. But this species has been known to bite humans.

Another mystery surrounding the nurse shark is the way in which it gives birth.

Usually female nurse sharks allow their eggs to hatch and grow inside their bodies. The young sharks then come out from their mother's womb alive and swimming. But scientists have seen the nurse shark release its eggs directly into the water. The eggs drift along and eventually hatch into the sea.

Because it lives on the mucky bottom of the ocean, the nurse shark must be able to breathe water without inhaling mud and other debris. To do this, nurse sharks pull water into special holes above their eyes. These cavities, called spiracles, filter out debris, while allowing water to enter the shark's gills.

Shortfin Mako Shark
Isurus oxyrinchus

Length: up to 13 feet
Weight: up to 1,300 pounds
Diet: fish, especially herring and mackerel
Home: worldwide in temperate and tropical oceans

Order: mackerel sharks
Family: mackerel sharks, porbeagles

Oceans and Shores

Fish

© AMOS NACHOUM / CORBIS

The shortfin mako shark is a strong, fierce predator that swims fast and shows no mercy toward its prey. Its streamlined body allows the creature to move rapidly through the open ocean. It often attains speeds of up to 40 miles per hour. If herring or mackerel could talk, they might tell you just how large the mako shark's mouth is. The shark likes to swallow its prey whole. It will also attack large fish, including the dangerous swordfish. Some makos have been found with entire swordfish in their stomachs!

Like all sharks, the mako doesn't have a single bone in its body. Its whole skeleton is made of cartilage. The mako's eyes are small but able to see well in dim light. Its most important sense, however, is smell. As the shark swims, water enters its two nostrils, carrying the smell of food.

After a male and female mako mate, the fertilized eggs remain in the female's body. There is enough food in the eggs for the developing babies. When a baby shark hatches, it leaves its mother's body and is ready to swim and eat on its own. In fact, the baby had better swim away quickly—it may be eaten by its hungry mother!

Makos are popular among sport fishermen. They often put up a fight and make spectacular leaps when they are hooked. Mako shark is considered a delicious food fish and is often served as a substitute for swordfish.

Small-Spotted Cat Shark
Scyliorhinus canicula

Length: up to 39 inches
Diet: mollusks, crustaceans, worms, and small fish
Method of Reproduction: egg layer

Home: eastern Atlantic Ocean
Order: ground sharks
Family: cat sharks

 Oceans and Shores

 Fish

© PAUL KAY / OSF / ANIMALS ANIMALS / EARTH SCENES

This beautiful, small shark is no danger to humans. In the past its skin was dried and used as sandpaper. But the skin is not as rough as that of most sharks. This shark is sometimes called a "dogfish" for its habit of hunting for food in "packs," as wild dogs do.

The small-spotted cat shark is one of the best-known European sharks. It prefers to live along the sandy bottom of coastal waters. Near the British Isles, small-spotted cat sharks are caught commercially and eaten either fresh or salted. They are also processed to make shark oil and fish meal.

Small-spotted cat sharks often gather in separate-sex groups. The female schools travel to their spawning grounds in early winter. The males join them in early spring. Then, in summer, the sharks form pairs and move into deep waters to mate. Some kinds of sharks give birth to live young, and others produce eggs. The small-spotted cat shark is an egg layer. The female has two egg tubes and lays one egg at a time—from one tube and then from the other. Most eggs are laid between November and July.

The egg of the small-spotted cat shark emerges in a hard, nearly transparent case covered with long threads. The threads tangle around seaweed in shallow water. Anchored in place, the egg continues to develop for 5 to 11 months. Most small-spotted cat sharks hatch after 8 or 9 months.

Tiger Shark
Galeocerdo cuvier

Length: up to 18 feet
Weight: up to 1,800 pounds
Diet: fish, sea turtles, and
    other marine life
Number of Young: up to 80

Home: Atlantic, Indian, and
    Pacific oceans
Order: ground sharks
Family: requiem sharks

Oceans and
Shores

Fish

© TOM BRAKEFIELD / CORBIS

The tiger shark is one of the ocean's most fearsome and fearless sharks. It will attack poisonous stingrays and fight with crocodiles. It will snatch seagulls paddling on the water's surface and make a meal of a large sea lion. To satisfy its voracious appetite, the tiger shark also eats sea turtles, crabs, porpoises, other sharks, and many other fish. Add to this amazing smorgasbord such oddities as leather wallets, copper wire, and cans of salmon—all of which have been found in the bellies of tiger sharks. This shark is a scavenger.

During the day, tiger sharks usually remain offshore in the warm, deep ocean waters. At night, six or so sharks gather in a pack and enter the shallow coastal waters to hunt. They are human-eaters and feared throughout the world.

Tiger sharks are hunted for many reasons. Their meat is eaten as steak. Their fins are used in soup. Their skin is made into leather. Their teeth are strung into necklaces. Shark-liver oil is a source of vitamin A in pills and ointments and is an ingredient in many lipsticks.

Young tiger sharks hatch from eggs while still inside their mother. The female gives birth to as many as 80 live pups, each about 2 feet long. The markings of the young tiger sharks give this species its name. They are born with black spots that change to stripes and then fade with age.

Whale Shark
Rhincodon typus

Length: up to 60 feet
Weight: about 22 tons
Diet: small crustaceans, fish, and squid
Method of Reproduction: gives birth to live young

Home: warm seas around the world
Order: carpet sharks
Family: whale sharks

 Oceans and Shores

Fish

© AMOS NACHOUM / CORBIS

The whale shark has the distinction of being the world's largest fish. A typical 40-foot-long specimen weighs in at an astounding 45,000 pounds! The whale shark seems to do everything in a big way. The female's eggs remain in her body. She gives birth to live young.

Despite its threatening name, the whale shark is not dangerous to humans. In fact, the whale shark doesn't attack or eat any big creatures. Instead, it feeds on plankton and other small organisms. It must devour enormous amounts of plankton to meet the needs of its huge body. A whale shark has thousands of tiny hooked teeth in its wide mouth. The teeth are arranged in more than 300 rows. And each row consists of

hundreds of teeth. The gills are covered with a webbing. This forms a sievelike mesh that strains out food as water passes through the mouth, over the gills, and back out into the sea.

The whale shark usually lives in the open ocean far from shore. It often joins with others of its kind to form groups, or schools. The creature swims slowly along the surface. Sometimes it even sleeps as it floats, bobbing up and down with the waves. As it feeds, the shark may "stand," taking a vertical position in the water. In this particular pose, its head rises above the surface while the tail hangs straight downward.

Bighorn Sheep
Ovis canadensis

Length: 4 to 6 feet
Weight: 200 to 300 pounds
Length of Horns: up to 40 inches
Diet: grass
Number of Young: 1

Home: western North America
Order: even-toed hoofed mammals
Family: antelope, bison, buffalo, cattle, goats, and sheep

 Forests and Mountains

 Mammals

© KENNAN WARD / CORBIS

Bighorn sheep are named for the huge curved horns of the rams (males). Females have smaller, slightly curved horns. Males use their horns in battles to decide who is strongest in a herd. Fortunately, these are not fights to the death. In fact, the males do battle without harming each other. Two male bighorns typically charge at each other head-on. They crash their horns together with a sound that echoes for miles. Next they may kick at one another. Then they stop to eat some grass. The fighters repeat this process until one gives up by allowing the winner to have the last kick.

Male bighorns spend most of the year in groups. They are separate from the females and young sheep. Most of the battles take place just before the males join the female herd for the mating season. Female bighorns are pregnant for six months. They give birth in the winter or spring. Young males stay with their mothers in the female herd for about 15 months. Then they join a male group.

Who are the bighorn sheep's greatest enemies? They're mountain lions, coyotes, gray foxes, and bobcats. Like guards in a tower, males often climb to high points on a mountain or ledge. From there they can see their enemies approach. When in danger, bighorns display their speed, agility, and endurance.

Common Shrimp
Crangon crangon

Length: up to 3½ inches
Diet: crustaceans, worms, and mollusks
Method of Reproduction: egg layer
Home: northeastern Atlantic Ocean and Mediterranean Sea

Order: crabs, crayfishes, lobsters, prawns, and shrimp
Family: sand shrimps

 Oceans and Shores

 Arthropods

© CHRISTIAN LEROY / BIOS / PETER ARNOLD, INC.

The medium-sized common shrimp is harvested in huge numbers from the North Sea and the central Mediterranean Sea. Germany, the Netherlands, Belgium, and Great Britain have large fishing fleets dedicated to catching this crustacean. Typically fishermen cook the shrimp on board their vessels. Very small shrimp are cooked and sold whole. Large ones are cooked and peeled. And then only the tail is eaten. The meat has a mild flavor and is popular throughout northern Europe.

The common shrimp lives at the sea bottom. It burrows into the sand and mud, leaving only its antennae visible above the dirt. In this way the shrimp avoids its many natural predators, including herring and tuna. At night, it emerges from hiding and scavenges along the ocean floor. The shrimp's front legs end in small claws. It uses these to pick up food.

These shrimp mate at night. The male releases his sperm. The female stores them until she is ready to lay and fertilize her eggs. She then tucks her clutch of eggs under her body. She carries them there until they hatch. The newborn shrimp larva is a tiny, buglike creature. Its body must undergo several transformations before it begins to resemble that of a small adult shrimp. Like other crustaceans, the common shrimp never stops growing. It must replace its hard outer skin at least once a year.

Northern Pink Shrimp
Penaeus duorarum

Length: 8½ inches (female); 6½ inches (male)

Diet: plant and animal matter, including decaying substances

Method of Reproduction: egg layer

Home: coastal waters from Maryland to Brazil

Order: crabs, crayfishes, lobsters, prawns, and shrimp

Family: prawns

 Oceans and Shores

 Arthropods

© DAVID S. ADDISON / VISUALS UNLIMITED

Many fish and other sea animals eat Northern pink shrimp. So do people. Commercial fishermen catch many tons of pink shrimp every year. Like all shrimp, the pink variety has three body parts: head, thorax, and abdomen. It has ten pairs of legs: five pairs of walking legs on the thorax, and five pairs of swimming legs on the abdomen. The shrimp swims by paddling with its swimming legs and rapidly bending its abdomen and tail back and forth. If a pink shrimp is grabbed by the tip of one of its legs, the leg detaches from its body. The attacker has the leg, but the shrimp gets away. The shrimp can easily regrow the lost leg.

Northern pink shrimp have a tough outer covering called the exoskeleton. In order to grow, a shrimp has to shed its exoskeleton, a process called molting. The old exoskeleton splits along the back, and the shrimp wiggles out. A new exoskeleton has already formed underneath the old one. At first, it is soft. The shrimp can grow quite a bit bigger before the new exoskeleton hardens.

Northern pink shrimp live on the ocean bottom, from very shallow water to depths of 300 feet. The eggs are laid some distance offshore. They hatch into tiny larvae that are carried toward shore by water currents. There the larvae live and grow in grassy bays and sounds. They pass through several stages before they become adults and move to deeper water.

Sidewinder
Crotalus cerastes

Length: 17 to 30 inches
Diet: small mammals and birds
Number of Young: 7 to 13
Home: southwestern United States and northern Mexico

Order: scaled reptiles
Family: pit vipers, vipers

 Deserts

© RICHARD CUMMINS / CORBIS

Reptiles

The sidewinder cannot slither like most snakes, because it lives in the desert. A snake trying to slither across the sand would just move sand from side to side. The snake itself would stay in one place. Instead, the sidewinder picks its head and tail up off the ground and moves them sideways. Then it shifts its weight onto its head and tail. And the rest of its body follows. It repeats this process again and again while undulating. This sounds complicated, but it allows the sidewinder to move a very efficient 2 miles per hour. That's pretty fast for a snake!

Sidewinders travel and hunt only at night. At midday the scorching desert sun could prove deadly in less than ten minutes. To help them in their nighttime hunting, sidewinders have a kind of sixth sense. Between their nostrils and eyes, they have small pits that enable them to sense warm objects. This "head detector" helps sidewinders pinpoint the location of a live mouse or bird standing as far as a foot and a half away. They catch their prey by suddenly striking out with their fangs.

The sidewinder's closest relative is the rattlesnake. Like rattlesnakes, sidewinders have venom in their fangs. They also have rattles on the ends of their tails. These warn other animals or people not to come too close. A sidewinder's bite can be harmful to humans.

Blue Skate
Dipturus batis

Length: up to 8¼ feet
Weight: up to 200 pounds
Diet: other fish and crustaceans
Method of Reproduction: egg layer

Home: eastern Atlantic Ocean and the Mediterranean Sea
Order: rays, sawfishes
Family: rays, skates

Oceans and Shores

Fish

The blue skate is a familiar fish in European waters. It is an enemy of codfish. It prowls the ocean bottom. There it eats other rays and flatfish such as flounder. It also consumes shellfish such as lobsters and crabs. Sometimes it leaves the bottom of the ocean to catch fish that swim at higher levels. It has a large appetite. But the blue skate usually finds all the food it needs in a very small area.

The skate is a large fish. So the adult skate's only serious enemies are the fishermen who trawl off the coast of northern Europe. The skate is also caught on very long fishing lines. Meat from the skate's "wings" is sold and eaten as fillets.

Blue skates have no scales. The young are very smooth to the touch. But as they mature, skates become very prickly. The adult female tends to be larger than her mate. She is also rougher—especially on her snout and front fins. Both sexes sport a row of spines down the middle of the tail.

After mating, the female skate does not shed her eggs right away. Inside her body hard capsules form around the eggs. They are released in spring and summer. By then these golden yellow egg cases are quite large. They have horns on the corners. These tangle in seaweed. The baby skate finishes developing inside its case. Then it must struggle fiercely to break out and swim free.

Eastern Spotted Skunk
Spilogale putorius

Length: 16 to 25 inches
Weight: 1 to 2½ pounds
Diet: small rodents, birds, reptiles, eggs, insects, worms, and fruits
Number of Young: 3 to 6

Home: eastern United States and Central America
Order: carnivores
Family: badgers, otters, skunks, weasels, and relatives

 Grasslands

 Mammals

© W. PERRY CONWAY / CORBIS

The eastern spotted skunk is a smaller, livelier version of its familiar cousin, the striped skunk. The spotted skunk is most active at night. It scrambles up trees and bounces from branch to branch. It is either chasing small animals or *being* chased by larger ones.

Like other skunks, the spotted skunk digs itself a burrow in the dirt. It will also take over the den of an animal it has killed. The spotted skunk is unlike its striped cousin in some ways. For example, it will nest in tree hollows high above the ground. It is also more social than most skunks. Several spotted skunks often cuddle together in one den during the coldest winter months.

When frightened or angered, the eastern spotted skunks sprays. It does this by turning its back and raising its hind end off the ground. Most animals will quickly retreat from this warning to avoid being bombarded with the skunk's infamous spray. This action does not save it from the great horned owl. This predator is the spotted skunk's number-one enemy. It swoops down from the sky without warning and snatches baby skunks from their mother.

Some scientists consider the eastern spotted skunk and its close cousin the western spotted skunk, *Spilogale gracilis*, to be part of the same species. The two breeds often mate when they meet in the middle of the country.

Slider
Trachemys scripta

Length: usually 5 to 8 inches
Diet: mainly aquatic plants
Method of Reproduction: egg layer
Home: central and southern United States south to northern South America; introduced elsewhere

Order: tortoises, turtles, and relatives
Family: box turtles and pond turtles

  Freshwater

Reptiles

© LYNDA RICHARDSON / CORBIS

The slider is a freshwater turtle that spends most of its life in water. Only occasionally does it climb onto land to bask in the warm sun. If anything disturbs it, the turtle quickly "slides" into nearby water and disappears from view.

It's easy to tell a male slider from a female slider. Just look at its fingers. Each of the slider's four limbs ends in four clawed fingers. In females, all the claws are about the same length. But in most males, the front claws are very long—about twice as long as the back claws.

Sliders live in muddy lakes, ponds, slow-moving rivers, swamps, and even large ditches. They are active during the daytime. The adults are vegetarians, feeding on various aquatic plants. Young sliders, however, eat a variety of foods. Their favorites are insects, snails, tadpoles, and other small animals.

After mating, a female slider crawls about looking for a good place to make a nest. She digs a hole with her back feet and lays her eggs in the hole. Then she covers the hole with soil. The eggs hatch in about two months. The baby sliders have very colorful carapaces (shells) only about 1¼ inches long. As sliders age, black spots appear on their carapaces. Over the years the shells become darker and darker, especially in males. In fact, the carapace of an old male may be almost entirely black!

Edible Snail
Helix pomatia

Height of the Shell: 1 to 2 inches
Diet: leaves
Number of Eggs: about 60

Home: Europe
Order: land snails and slugs
Family: typical snails

 Cities, Towns, and Farms

 Other Invertebrates

© HERBERT KEHRER / ZEFA / CORBIS

In France, the edible snail is called the Burgundy snail, after the area in France where it is often found. But it does not live only in Burgundy; it can also be found in much of Europe. It takes cover under plants in vineyards and gardens. There it can hide from its enemies—birds, rats, frogs, and people. The snail does not like heat or dryness and prefers to come out on rainy days.

When winter comes, the snail buries itself. It can burrow more than a foot below the surface if the ground is not too hard. Once buried, it falls into a deep sleep. When the ground warms up in the spring, the snail wakes up. When it rains, the snail becomes active again. It feeds for the first time in months, moving slowly under a rainy sky or in the cool of the night. If it is windy or too dry, it will hide in its shell and wait for better days.

Snails pair up in May or June. They prepare a hole in the ground where they lay their eggs. They grow very fast and can live up to five years. Snails have ridges on their shells, and you can count them to know how old a snail is.

Edible snails are much appreciated by food lovers. They have become scarce in some areas, so people try to raise them on snail farms. But this is not easy, because even though they're slow, they can still wander away.

Common Garter Snake
Thamnophis sirtalis

Length: 18 to 48 inches
Diet: amphibians, mice, birds, insects, and worms
Number of Young: 3 to 85
Home: United States and Canada

Order: scaled reptiles
Family: colubrids, typical snakes

 Cities, Towns, and Farms

 Reptiles

© JOE MCDONALD / CORBIS

For many North Americans, the garter snake is the only kind of snake they know. Fortunately, they need not worry. The garter snake is a harmless creature. It makes its home in fields, along roadsides, and around the foundations of houses. It is, in fact, one of the region's most common snakes. It can swim well, too. So swamps and streams are not a barrier to it. However, garter snakes must be careful not to get chilled in cold water. All snakes are cold-blooded. This means that they can't keep their internal temperature much warmer than their surroundings. As their body temperature drops, they begin to move more and more slowly. A garter snake swimming across a chilly pond or stream had better reach the other side before it

slows to a complete stop! In areas with cold winters, garter snakes hibernate. Sometime between October and early December, they crawl into holes 2 or 3 feet below the ground. Often several garter snakes share a winter burrow. They all snuggle together for warmth. They emerge from their holes in the spring.

A garter snake may mate in the fall, before beginning hibernation. Or it may do so in the spring, shortly after it emerges. Garter snakes give birth to live baby snakes, not eggs. But they are not true "live-bearers," as mammals are. Female garter snakes actually produce thin-shelled eggs and carry them inside their bodies. The eggs hatch just before the young snakes are born.

Eastern Ribbon Snake
Thamnophis sauritus

Length: 16 to 36 inches
Diet: insects, spiders, frogs, toads, mice, salamanders, and fish
Number of Young: 3 to 26

Home: eastern United States
Order: scaled reptiles
Family: colubrids, typical snakes

Forests and Mountains

Reptiles

© GARY MESZAROS / PHOTO RESEARCHERS

The eastern ribbon snake loves bogs, stream banks, and other moist places. It does not like hot, dry summers. To get away from the heat, it crawls underground and sleeps for days at a time. These long summertime naps are called "estivations." They are much like winter hibernation. In fact, the ribbon snake hibernates, too. It sleeps through harsh winter weather from the fall until early spring.

The eastern ribbon snake comes out of hibernation in March, April, or May. It has one thing on its mind—to find a mate! The ribbon snake is a relative of the garter snake. Like the garter snake, the ribbon snake produces eggs within its body, but never lays them. The eggs hatch inside the mother. The mother then gives birth to live young in July or August.

The ribbon snake uses both sight and smell to find food. It likes to eat small rodents, amphibians, fish, and insects. Ribbon snakes are prey to birds, mammals, and larger snakes. Young ribbon snakes have even more enemies. They are a favorite meal of fish, turtles, and crayfish.

Fortunately, ribbon snakes know how to defend themselves. They can spray their attackers with an unpleasant musk. Sometimes they also bite. If all else fails, the ribbon snake can shed its tail. A predator may then end up with only a mouthful of tail meat. While the predator is holding the tail, the snake escapes alive—if a bit shorter.

Red Snapper
Lutjanus campechanus

Length: up to 3 feet
Weight: up to 35 pounds
Diet: fish, crustaceans, and vegetation
Method of Reproduction: egg layer

Home: Gulf of Mexico and Caribbean Sea
Order: perch-like fishes
Family: fusiliers, sea perches

 Oceans and Shores

 Fish

© E. BRADLEY / PHOTEX / ZEFA / CORBIS

The red snapper is named for the way it suddenly and forcibly opens and shuts its jaws when dying. In this way, it has often seriously wounded unwary fishermen. The red snapper is a lovely rose color. Its mouth is large, and its teeth slope toward the corners. This gives the fish a grouchy look.

Red snappers are euryphagous. This means that they will try to swallow just about anything that moves. They prefer to eat smaller fish. But they will settle for crabs, squid, worms, mollusks, and algae. Snappers hunt mainly at night. They stalk their prey slowly, sneaking very close. Then suddenly they bite ferociously.

Snappers travel in large schools. They inhabit coral reefs and shallow waters. They usually remain near the coast during the summer and move offshore as fall arrives. They are thought to spawn in deep water during the fall.

The red snapper is a favorite seafood item. Unfortunately, this creature is one of about 300 species that can cause a painful type of food poisoning, called ciguatera. Scientists think ciguatera is caused when the red snapper eats a type of poisonous blue-green algae. The algae doesn't seem to hurt the fish. But people who eat a contaminated fish can suffer from severe cramping, diarrhea, and, in extreme cases, paralysis. Experts still don't know when or where a rare outbreak of ciguatera will strike.

Common Snipe
Gallinago gallinago

Length: 10 to 11 inches
Diet: insects, crustaceans, and mollusks
Number of Eggs: 3 to 4
Home: *Summer:* northern North America and Eurasia

Winter: southern United States south to Brazil; also Africa, India, and Indonesia
Order: auks, herons, and relatives
Family: sandpipers

 Cities, Towns, and Farms

 Birds

☐ Summer
■ Winter

© JOE MCDONALD / CORBIS

When we think of bird sounds, we usually think of singing. But some birds, such as the common snipe, also make sounds with their bills, feet, and feathers. During the mating season, the male snipe accompanies his courtship flight with a booming sound. This is made by air hitting his tail feathers. He makes the drumming noise while diving straight down over his prospective mate's head. This causes air to rush over two special feathers on either side of his tail.

Despite its dramatic breeding display, the common snipe is a shy, secretive bird that avoids humans. Its striped plumage provides camouflage in the marshes and wet meadows where it nests. This bird builds its nest on dry ground in clumps of tall grass. The bird pulls the grass over its nest to cover the olive brown eggs. The female sits on her eggs for 17 to 19 days. Her mate seldom helps incubate the eggs. But he does help guard the nest by trying to distract predators and humans with his showy flight.

Common snipe can be found all over the world. They live in marshes, wet meadows, and moors. Their numbers are declining in many places. But in cities, they have become somewhat more common in the past century. They like to nest on gravel rooftops. These were introduced in many towns in the mid-1800s.

House Sparrow
Passer domesticus

Length: up to 6 inches
Diet: insects, fruits, spiders, seeds, and blossoms
Number of Eggs: 3 to 7

Home: inhabited areas worldwide
Order: perching birds
Family: weavers, sparrows

  Cities, Towns, and Farms

 Birds

Everyone knows this sturdy little bird. The house sparrow has been living alongside people for ages. The partnership probably started when humans first began farming in the Middle East. The house sparrow grew fat and happy on the grain spread in the manure of domesticated cattle and horses. Not a picky eater, it also feasted on the crumbs found in human garbage. In return the house sparrow helped the farmer by gobbling up pesky insects and nibbling away at troublesome weeds.

In 1850 several New Yorkers decided to introduce this species to help control the worms and larvae that were destroying the plants in their parks and gardens. First, a cage of 8 sparrows was released into Central Park in New York City. This family did well for a while but eventually disappeared. Not giving up easily, Nicholas Pike of Brooklyn sailed to Liverpool, England, and brought back 100 house sparrows. Today the offspring of those birds have spread across the entire continent.

While house sparrows thrive in and around towns and farms, they do not do as well in natural environments, such as the thick forest or open desert. They are happiest living where human habitation produces garbage and weeds to eat. House sparrows are always eager for handouts. You can recognize the male of this species by his gray crown and black bib. His mate wears plain brown feathers.

Black Widow Spider
Latrodectus mactans

Length: ⅜ inch (female); ⅛ inch (male)
Diet: insects
Method of Reproduction: egg layer

Home: central and southern United States
Order: spiders
Family: cobweb weavers

Cities, Towns, and Farms

Arthropods

© BUDDY MAYS / CORBIS

The black widow spider's notorious reputation is only partially deserved. True, the female of the species packs a highly venomous (poisonous) bite. But fortunately, she bites only when defending her eggs. This spider is, in fact, extremely timid. This characteristic disproves the belief that the female black widow kills the male after mating. This myth may have arisen from the substantial size difference between the sexes. The female is three times bigger than the male.

There is, nonetheless, much to fear from black widow spiders. For starters, they favor cool, dark places. Their favorite hideouts are cellars, old buildings, and under porches. They are not visible there. And, of course,

there's really no way to know whether the female is protecting eggs. The venom from a black widow spider attacks the nervous system. It causes cramps, nausea, dizziness, and worse. Children seem to have the most serious reactions. Antidotes are available for black widow venom. But a full recovery from the effects may still take up to two months.

This spider has a characteristic red marking on its underside. The marking is shaped like an hourglass. Both sexes are jet black. The spider spins a coarse, irregularly shaped web. There the female spends nearly all her time. The newborn spiderlings receive no parental attention.

A

aardvark **1**:5
acorn woodpecker **10**:37
Adelie penguin **7**:18
African bullfrog **2**:11
African elephant **3**:36
African wild ass **1**:18
Alabama water dog **10**:17
albatross, wandering **1**:6
alligator, American **1**:7
alpine ibex **5**:7
Amazon dolphin **3**:21
American alligator **1**:7
American anhinga **1**:10
American bison **1**:37
American bumblebee **2**:12
American cockroach **2**:37
American horsefly **4**:42
American lobster **5**:34
American marten **6**:6
American mink **6**:8
American robin **7**:44
American toad **9**:32
amphibians
    bullfrog **2**:10
    bullfrog, African **2**:11
    frog, Cuban tree **4**:13
    frog, green **4**:14
    frog, poison dart **4**:15
    frog, wood **4**:16
    peeper, spring **7**:17
    toad, American **9**:32
    toad, western spadefoot **9**:33
    water dog, Alabama **10**:17
anaconda, green **1**:8
Andean condor **2**:39
angelfish **1**:9
anhinga, American **1**:10
ant, army **1**:11
ant, black carpenter **1**:12
ant, fire **1**:13
anteater, giant **1**:14
ant-eating woodpecker (acorn
    woodpecker) **10**:37
Arabian camel **2**:16
Arabian oryx **6**:37
archerfish **1**:15
Arctic char **2**:24
Arctic fox **4**:9
Arctic ground squirrel **9**:8
Arctic tern **9**:25
armadillo, screaming hairy **1**:16
armadillo lizard **5**:31
army ant **1**:11
arthropods
    ant, army **1**:11
    ant, black carpenter **1**:12
    ant, fire **1**:13
    bed bug **1**:32
    bee, honey **1**:33
    beetle, Japanese **1**:34
    bumblebee, American **2**:12
    butterfly, monarch **2**:13
    caterpillar, woolly bear **2**:22
    centipede, house **2**:23
    cicada, seventeen-year **2**:30
    cockroach, American **2**:37
    crab, Florida stone **3**:6
    crab, giant hermit **3**:7
    crab, horseshoe **3**:8
    cricket, house **3**:11
    daddy longlegs (harvestman)
      3:14
    fiddler, Atlantic marsh **3**:41
    firefly, North American **3**:42
    fly, tsetse **4**:8
    fruit fly, common **4**:7
    horsefly, American **4**:42
    lobster, American **5**:34
    lobster, Caribbean spiny **5**:35
    mantis, praying **5**:44
    mosquito **6**:22
    moth, Atlas **6**:23
    moth, gypsy **6**:24
    moth, luna **6**:25
    nymph, common wood **6**:31
    shrimp, common **8**:32
    shrimp, northern pink **8**:33
    spider, black widow **8**:44
    spider, garden **9**:5
    spider, house **9**:6
    spider, wolf **9**:7
    tarantula **9**:21
    tarantula, desert blond **9**:22
    termite, eastern subterranean
      9:24
    water bug, giant **10**:16
    weevil, boll **10**:19
    yellow jacket, eastern **10**:42
Asian cobra **2**:34
Asian dhole **3**:18
Asian elephant **3**:37
Asiatic black bear **1**:28
asp **1**:17
ass, African wild **1**:18
Atlantic herring **4**:37
Atlantic marsh fiddler **3**:41
Atlantic puffin **7**:29
Atlantic razor clam **2**:31
Atlantic salmon **8**:6
Atlantic stingray **9**:13
Atlantic walrus **10**:12
Atlas moth **6**:23
aye-aye **1**:19

B

baboons
    chacma **1**:20
    gelada **1**:21
    hamadryas **1**:22
    yellow **1**:23
Bactrian camel **2**:17
badger, Eurasian **1**:24
bald eagle **3**:32
ball python **7**:31
banded linsang **5**:29
banded mongoose **6**:11
bandicoot, spiny **1**:25
Barbary macaque **5**:38
barn owl **6**:42
barn swallow **9**:15
barracuda, great **1**:26
bass, striped **1**:27
bay scallop **8**:12
bearded pig **7**:24
bearded seal **8**:18
bears
    Asiatic black **1**:28
    black **1**:29
    brown **1**:30
    panda, giant **7**:9
    panda, red **7**:10
    polar **1**:31
bed bug **1**:32
bee, honey **1**:33
beetle, Japanese **1**:34
beluga **1**:35
Bengal tiger **9**:28
bighorn sheep **8**:31
bird-eating spider (tarantula) **9**:21
bird of paradise, blue **1**:36
birds
    albatross, wandering **1**:6
    anhinga, American **1**:10
    blackbird, red-winged **1**:38
    bluebird, eastern **1**:39
    bluebird, mountain **1**:40
    blue bird of paradise **1**:36
    bobolink **2**:5
    booby, masked **2**:7
    booby, red-footed **2**:8
    bufflehead **2**:9
    buzzard, common **2**:14
    cardinal **2**:20
    cockatiel **2**:35
    cockatoo, sulphur-crested **2**:36
    condor, Andean **2**:39
    condor, California **2**:40
    crane, common **3**:9
    crane, whooping **3**:10
    dove, white-winged **3**:27
    duck, mandarin **3**:29
    duck, ruddy **3**:30
    duck, wood **3**:31
    eagle, bald **3**:32
    egret, snowy **3**:35
    falcon, peregrine **3**:38
    flamingo, greater **4**:6
    goose, Canada **4**:25
    goose, snow **4**:26
    grosbeak, evening **4**:28

grosbeak, rose-breasted **4**:29
gull, laughing **4**:31
heron, great blue **4**:35
heron, green-backed **4**:36
hornbill, great **4**:40
hornbill, rhinoceros **4**:41
hummingbird, broad-tailed
    4:43
hummingbird, ruby-throated
    4:44
ibis, scarlet **5**:8
jay, blue **5**:14
kingfisher **5**:18
kookaburra **5**:21
loon, common **5**:36
mallard **5**:40
meadowlark, eastern **6**:7
mockingbird **6**:9
nightingale **6**:30
oriole, golden **6**:36
osprey **6**:38
ostrich **6**:39
owl, barn **6**:42
owl, boreal **6**:43
owl, great horned **6**:44
owl, pygmy **7**:5
owl, screech **7**:6
owl, snowy **7**:7
parakeet, monk **7**:12
parrot, yellow-headed **7**:13
peafowl, Indian **7**:16
penguin, Adelie penguin **7**:18
penguin, chinstrap **7**:19
penguin, king **7**:20
penguin, little blue **7**:21
penguin, Magellanic **7**:22
pheasant, ring-necked **7**:23
pigeon, passenger **7**:25
pintail **7**:26
puffin, Atlantic **7**:29
quail, common **7**:32
raven, common **7**:37
rhea, Darwin's **7**:38
roadrunner, greater **7**:43
robin, American **7**:44
sandpiper, common **8**:10
sapsucker, yellow-bellied **8**:11
snipe, common **8**:42
sparrow, house **8**:43
starling, common **9**:12
swallow, barn **9**:15
swallow, cliff **9**:16
swan, black **9**:17
swan, trumpeter **9**:18
tern, Arctic **9**:25
tern, common **9**:26
titmouse, tufted **9**:31
toucan, toco **9**:36
turkey **9**:40
turkey, Latham's brush **9**:41
turtledove **10**:9
vulture, turkey **10**:11
warbler, Tennessee **10**:14
whippoorwill **10**:32
woodpecker, acorn **10**:37
woodpecker, ivory-billed
    10:38
woodpecker, red-headed **10**:39
wren, house **10**:40
bison, American **1**:37
black bear **1**:29
black bear, Asiatic **1**:28
blackbird, red-winged **1**:38
black carpenter ant **1**:12
black-footed ferret **3**:40
black howler monkey **6**:12
black rhinoceros **7**:39
black spider monkey **6**:13
black swan **9**:17
black widow spider **8**:44
blond tarantula, desert **9**:22
bluebird, eastern **1**:39
bluebird, mountain **1**:40
blue bird of paradise **1**:36
bluefin tuna **9**:39
bluefish **1**:41
blue heron, great **4**:35
blue jay **5**:14
blue limpet **5**:28
blue monkey **6**:14
blue shark **8**:24

blue skate **8**:35
blue whale **10**:20
boa, emerald tree **1**:43
boa constrictor **1**:42
bobcat **1**:44
bobolink **2**:5
boll weevil **10**:19
bonefish **2**:6
booby, masked **2**:7
booby, red-footed **2**:8
boreal owl **6**:43
bottle-nosed dolphin **3**:22
box turtle, common **9**:42
box turtle, ornate **10**:6
brain coral **2**:42
Brazilian tapir **9**:20
brindled gnu (wildebeest) **4**:23
broad-tailed hummingbird **4**:43
brown bear **1**:30
brown hyena **5**:5
brown lemur **5**:24
brush turkey, Latham's **9**:41
bufflehead **2**:9
bug, bed **1**:32
bullfrog **2**:10
bullfrog, African **2**:11
bumblebee, American **2**:12
Burgundy snail (edible snail)
    8:38
butterflies *see also* moths
    monarch **2**:13
    nymph, common wood **6**:31
buzzard, common **2**:14

C

caiman, dwarf **2**:15
California condor **2**:40
California moray **6**:21
California sea lion **8**:15
camel, Arabian **2**:16
camel, Bactrian **2**:17
Canada goose **4**:25
Canadian lynx **5**:37
Canadian otter **6**:40
cape pangolin **7**:11
capuchin, white-throated **2**:18
caracal **2**:19
cardinal **2**:20
Caribbean spiny lobster **5**:35
carpenter ant, black **1**:12
cat, sand **2**:21
catamount (puma) **7**:30
caterpillar, woolly bear **2**:22
centipede, house **2**:23
chacma baboon **1**:20
channeled whelk **10**:31
char, Arctic **2**:24
cheetah **2**:25
cheetah, king **2**:26
chimpanzee **2**:27
chimpanzee, pygmy **2**:28
chinchilla **2**:29
chinook salmon **8**:7
chinstrap penguin **7**:19
cicada, seventeen-year **2**:30
clam, Atlantic razor **2**:31
clam, giant **2**:32
clam, soft-shelled **2**:33
cliff swallow **9**:16
clown fish **3**:43
cobra, Asian **2**:34
cockatiel **2**:35
cockatoo, sulphur-crested **2**:36
cockroach, American **2**:37
Commerson's dolphin **3**:23
common, for names beginning
    see next part of name
conch, queen **2**:38
condor, Andean **2**:39
condor, California **2**:40
constrictor, boa **1**:42
copperhead **2**:41
coral, brain **2**:42
coral, large flower **2**:43
cottonmouth **2**:44
cougar (puma) **7**:30
coyote **3**:5
crabs
    Atlantic marsh fiddler **3**:41
    Florida stone **3**:6